oust rift lash ... ... lea

year gul... ... c

took pawn ague edit claw

neon hymn wren pair

gift wire pelt

A
READER'S
JOURNAL

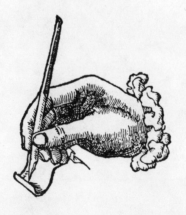

A READER'S JOURNAL

PROSPERO
B·O·O·K·S
A DIVISION OF CHAPTERS INC.

ISBN 1-55110-697-3
© Copyright 1997 held by   Chapters Inc.
90 Ronson Drive
Etobicoke, Ontario
M9W 1C1

This edition produced for Prospero Books,
a division of Chapters Inc.
by Waterlane Editions
Vancouver, Toronto

Printed and bound in Canada by Friesens, Altona, Manitoba.

Canadian Cataloguing in Publication Data
Main entry under title:

A reader's diary

Co-published by: Prospero Books.
ISBN 1-55110-698-1 (Waterlane) – ISBN 1-55110-697-3 (Prospero)

1. Books and reading. 2. Diaries (Blank-books)
PN4395R42 1997   O28'9   C97-910692-3

TABLE OF CONTENTS

GREAT EXPECTATIONS 7
where we record the books we would like to read, listed by title, author and subject

A ROOM OF ONE'S OWN 29
where we record the books we would like to add to our personal library

SENSE AND SENSIBILITY 39
in which we find a detailed record of thoughts and impressions on books we have read

KIDNAPPED 75
in which we find lists of the books we have borrowed and those borrowed from us

FATHERS AND SONS 89
in which we find lists of books to give as gifts and those books given to us

WHEN WE WERE VERY YOUNG 107
in which we remember our favourite children's books, from youth and adulthood

ON THE ROAD 111
in which we find a collection of books suited for holidays, beaches and buses

FAR FROM THE MADDING CROWD 115
in which we make note of book festivals, author readings and other events for readers

A CIRCLE OF FRIENDS 121
in which we find a list of members of our reading club, lists of books to read in a group and the thoughts of the group on books read

THE MERCHANT OF VENICE 135
in which we find addresses of bookstores, libraries, and book-loving friends

FAMOUS LAST WORDS 141
in which we record memorable quotations from favourite books and authors

EX · · ·   LIBRIS

GREAT
EXPECTATIONS
where we record the books we would like to read,
listed by title, author and subject

A truly great book should be read in youth, once again in maturity and once more in old age, as a fine building should be seen by morning light, at noon and by moonlight.

Robertson Davies (1913-95)

F or one who reads, there is no limit to the
   number of lives that may be lived, for fiction,
biography, and history offer an inexhaustible
number of lives in many parts of the world, in all
periods of time.

Louis L'Amour (1908-88)

W
here is human nature so weak as in the bookstore!
Henry Ward Beecher (1813-87)

Without books, history is silent, literature dumb, science crippled, thought and speculation at a standstill.

Barbara Tuchman (1912-89)

When writers die they become books, which is, afterall, not too bad an incarnation.

Jorge Luis Borges (1899-1986)

The only books that influence us are those for which we are ready, and which have gone a little farther down our particular path than we have yet got ourselves.

E.M. Forster (1879-1970)

A bad book is as much a labour
to write as a good book.
Aldous Huxley (1894-1963)

There is only one trait that marks the writer. He is always watching. It's a kind of trick of the mind and he is born with it.

Morley Callaghan (1903-90)

There is no money in poetry, but then
there's no poetry in money either.
Robert Graves (1895-1985)

A ROOM OF ONE'S OWN

where we record the books we would like to add to our personal library

title

author

publisher/pub.date

notes

title

author

publisher/pub.date

notes

title

author

publisher/pub.date

notes

title

author

publisher/pub.date

notes

A s sheer casual reading matter, I still
find the English dictionary the most
interesting book in our language.

Albert Jay Nock (1873-1945)

title
_____

author
_____

publisher/pub.date
_____

notes
_____

title
_____

author
_____

publisher/pub.date
_____

notes
_____

title
_____

author
_____

publisher/pub.date
_____

notes
_____

title
_____

author
_____

publisher/pub.date
_____

notes
_____

title
_____

author
_____

publisher/pub.date
_____

notes
_____

title

author

publisher/pub. date

notes

title

author

publisher/pub. date

notes

title

author

publisher/pub. date

notes

title

author

publisher/pub. date

notes

title

author

publisher/pub. date

notes

title

author

publisher/pub.date

notes

title

author

publisher/pub.date

notes

title

author

publisher/pub.date

notes

title

author

publisher/pub.date

notes

title

author

publisher/pub.date

notes

title
_____

author
_____

publisher/pub.date
_____

notes
_____

title
_____

author
_____

publisher/pub.date
_____

notes
_____

title
_____

author
_____

publisher/pub.date
_____

notes
_____

title
_____

author
_____

publisher/pub.date
_____

notes
_____

title
_____

author
_____

publisher/pub.date
_____

notes
_____

Fundamentally, all writing is about the same thing: it's about dying, about the brief flicker of time we have here, and the frustration that it creates.

Mordecai Richler (1931-)

title

author

publisher/pub.date

notes

title

author

publisher/pub.date

notes

title

author

publisher/pub.date

notes

title

author

publisher/pub.date

notes

title

author

publisher/pub.date

notes

title

author

publisher/pub.date

notes

title

author

publisher/pub.date

notes

title

author

publisher/pub.date

notes

title

author

publisher/pub.date

notes

title

author

publisher/pub.date

notes

title

author

publisher/pub.date

notes

title

author

publisher/pub.date

notes

title

author

publisher/pub.date

notes

All good books have one thing in common – they are truer than if they had really happened, and after you've read one of them you will feel that all that happened, happened to you and that it belongs to you forever....

Ernest Hemingway (1899-1961)

title

author

publisher/pub.date

notes

---

title

author

publisher/pub.date

notes

---

title

author

publisher/pub.date

notes

---

title

author

publisher/pub.date

notes

SENSE AND SENSIBILITY

*in which we find a detailed record of thoughts
and impressions on books we have read*

title   A CIVIL ACTION (GIFT FROM MOM)

author   JONATHAN HARR

date and place read   VANDERHOOF, 100 MILE HOUSE, RICHMON

notes   A VERY FAST PACED READ ON A TRUE
STORY. VERY WELL WRITTEN, ALL SIDES
PARTICIPATING. HARD TO BELIEVE
JUSTICE WAS SERVED. . . .

title   THE CHAMBER

author   JOHN GRISHAM

date and place read   JAN – FEB 1999   RICHMOND

notes   VERY DARK AND DISTURBING
PICTURE OF LIFE ON DEATH ROW.
NO MATTER WHICH SIDE YOU SIT ON
NO PAT ANSWERS

ow many a man has dated a new era in his life from
the reading of a book! The book exists for us,
perchance, that will explain our miracles and reveal new
ones. The at present unutterable things we may find
somewhere uttered.

Henry David Thoreau (1817-62)

title ISAACS STORM

author

date and place read VEGAS, THE HILLS JUNE - JULY 01 + HOME

notes MIXING FACT + FICTION AN INTERESTING TALE ABOUT WHAT IS TRUE + WHAT WHAT WE WANT TO BELIEVE

title EAST OF THE MOUNTAINS

author DAVID GUTERSON

date and place read SEPTEMBER '99 AT HOME

notes VERY WELL WRITTEN STORY OF A MAN'S JOURNEY TO ONE PLACE IN WHICH HE ARRIVES SOMEWERE ELSE ENTIRELY.

title REMAINS OF THE DAY

author KAZUO ISHIGURO

date and place read DEC - JAN AT HOME

notes A STORY THAT IS A METAPHOR FOR MANY THINGS IN OUR LIVES AND HOW WE COPE WITH WHAT WE HAD PLANNED + WHAT ACTUALLY HAPPENED.

title WHEN WE WERE ORPHANS

author KAZUO ISHIGURO

date and place read JULY - DEC 00   AT HOME

notes THE AUTHORS PROSE BATTLES WITH
HIS CHARACTERS IDIOSYNCRASYES FOR
SUPREMACY IN THE READERS MIND.

title ON CHESIL BEACH

author IAN MCEWAN

date and place read SEPT 2016 -

notes

title

author

date and place read

notes

title

author

date and place read

notes

title A.H.W.S.G.

author DAVE EGGERS

date and place read

notes

title

author

date and place read

notes

title

author

date and place read

notes

title

author

date and place read

notes

title

author

date and place read

notes

title

author

date and place read

notes

title

author

date and place read

notes

title

author

date and place read

notes

 ome books are to be tasted, others to be swallowed, and some to be chewed and digested.

Francis Bacon (1561-1626)

title

author

date and place read

notes

_____

_____

_____

_____

title

author

date and place read

notes

_____

_____

_____

_____

title

author

date and place read

notes

_____

_____

_____

_____

title

author

date and place read

notes

_____

_____

_____

title

author

date and place read

notes

_____

_____

_____

title

author

date and place read

notes

_____

_____

_____

L iterature is my Utopia. Here I am not disfranchised. No barrier of the senses shuts me out from the sweet, gracious discourse of my book friends. They talk to me without embarrassment or awkwardness.

Helen Keller (1880-1968)

title

author

date and place read

notes

title

author

date and place read

notes

title
_____

author
_____

date and place read
_____

notes
_____

_____

_____

_____

title
_____

author
_____

date and place read
_____

notes
_____

_____

_____

_____

title
_____

author
_____

date and place read
_____

notes
_____

_____

_____

_____

title

author

date and place read

notes

title

author

date and place read

notes

title

author

date and place read

notes

title

author

date and place read

notes

_____

_____

_____

_____

title

author

date and place read

notes

_____

_____

_____

_____

title

author

date and place read

notes

_____

_____

_____

title

author

date and place read

notes

title

author

date and place read

notes

title

author

date and place read

notes

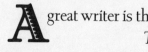

great writer is the friend and benefactor of his readers.
Thomas Babington Macaulay (1800-59)

title

author

date and place read

notes

title

author

date and place read

notes

title

author

date and place read

notes

title

author

date and place read

notes

title

author

date and place read

notes

title

author

date and place read

notes

title

author

date and place read

notes

title

author

date and place read

notes

title

author

date and place read

notes

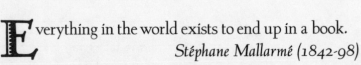

Everything in the world exists to end up in a book.
Stéphane Mallarmé (1842-98)

title

author

date and place read

notes

title

author

date and place read

notes

title

author

date and place read

notes

title

author

date and place read

notes

_____

_____

_____

title

author

date and place read

notes

_____

_____

_____

title

author

date and place read

notes

_____

_____

_____

L iterature is where I go to explore the highest and lowest places in human society and in the human spirit, where I hope to find out not the absolute truth but the truth of the tale, of the imagination and of the heart.

Salman Rushdie (1947-)

title

author

date and place read

notes

title

author

date and place read

notes

title

author

date and place read

notes

title

author

date and place read

notes

title

author

date and place read

notes

title

author

date and place read

notes

title

author

date and place read

notes

title

author

date and place read

notes

title

author

date and place read

notes

title

author

date and place read

notes

title

author

date and place read

notes

 hile thought exists, words are alive and literature
becomes an escape, not from, but into living.

Cyril Connolly (1903-74)

title
_____

author
_____

date and place read
_____

notes
_____

_____

_____

_____

title
_____

author
_____

date and place read
_____

notes
_____

_____

_____

_____

title
_____

author
_____

date and place read
_____

notes
_____

_____

_____

_____

title

author

date and place read

notes

title

author

date and place read

notes

title

author

date and place read

notes

title

author

date and place read

notes

title

author

date and place read

notes

title

author

date and place read

notes

Writing is no trouble: you just jot down ideas as they occur to you. The jotting is simplicity itself – it is the occurring which is difficult.

Stephen Leacock (1869-1944)

title

author

date and place read

notes

title

author

date and place read

notes

title

author

date and place read

notes

title

author

date and place read

notes

title

author

date and place read

notes

title

author

date and place read

notes

title

author

date and place read

notes

title

author

date and place read

notes

title

author

date and place read

notes

title

author

date and place read

notes

title

author

date and place read

notes

title

author

date and place read

notes

title

author

date and place read

notes

title

author

date and place read

notes

title

author

date and place read

notes

 book is solitude, privacy; it is a way of holding the self apart from the crush of the outer world.

Sven Birkerts (1951-)

title
_____

author
_____

date and place read
_____

notes
_____

_____

_____

_____

title
_____

author
_____

date and place read
_____

notes
_____

_____

_____

_____

title
_____

author
_____

date and place read
_____

notes
_____

_____

_____

_____

title

author

date and place read

notes

title

author

date and place read

notes

title

author

date and place read

notes

title
_____

author
_____

date and place read
_____

notes
_____

_____

_____

_____

title
_____

author
_____

date and place read
_____

notes
_____

_____

_____

_____

title
_____

author
_____

date and place read
_____

notes
_____

I t is a great thing to start life with a small number of
really good books which are your very own.

Sir Arthur Conan Doyle (1859-1930)

title

author

date and place read

notes

title

author

date and place read

notes

title

author

date and place read

notes

title

author

date and place read

notes

title

author

date and place read

notes

EX LIBRIS

KIDNAPPED
in which we find lists of books
we have borrowed and those borrowed from us

title

author

borrowed from

date borrowed

date returned

title

author

borrowed from

date borrowed

date returned

title

author

borrowed from

date borrowed

date returned

title

author

borrowed from

date borrowed

date returned

KIDNAPPED *books we have borrowed* —

A room without books is like a body without soul.
Marcus Tullius Cicero (106-43 BC)

title
_____

author
_____

borrowed from
_____

date borrowed
_____

date returned
_____

title
_____

author
_____

borrowed from
_____

date borrowed
_____

date returned
_____

title
_____

author
_____

borrowed from
_____

date borrowed
_____

date returned
_____

title

author

borrowed from

date borrowed

date returned

title

author

borrowed from

date borrowed

date returned

title

author

borrowed from

date borrowed

date returned

title

author

borrowed from

date borrowed

date returned

title

author

borrowed from

date borrowed

date returned

title

author

borrowed from

date borrowed

date returned

title

author

borrowed from

date borrowed

date returned

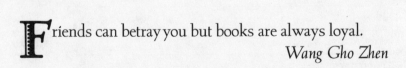

Friends can betray you but books are always loyal.
Wang Gho Zhen

title

author

borrowed from

date borrowed

date returned

title

author

borrowed from

date borrowed

date returned

title

author

borrowed from

date borrowed

date returned

title

author

borrowed from

date borrowed

date returned

title

author

borrowed from

date borrowed

date returned

title

author

borrowed from

date borrowed

date returned

title

author

borrowed from

date borrowed

date returned

title

author

borrowed from

date borrowed

date returned

title

author

borrowed by

date borrowed

date returned

title

author

borrowed by

date borrowed

date returned

title

author

borrowed by

date borrowed

date returned

Every man who knows how to read has it in his power to magnify himself, to multiply the ways in which he exists, to make his life full, significant and interesting.

Aldous Huxley (1894-1963)

title

author

borrowed by

date borrowed

date returned

title

author

borrowed by

date borrowed

date returned

title

author

borrowed by

date borrowed

date returned

title

author

borrowed by

date borrowed

date returned

title

author

borrowed by

date borrowed

date returned

title

author

borrowed by

date borrowed

date returned

title

author

borrowed by

date borrowed

date returned

title

author

borrowed by

date borrowed

date returned

title
_____

author
_____

borrowed by
_____

date borrowed
_____

date returned
_____

title
_____

author
_____

borrowed by
_____

date borrowed
_____

date returned
_____

title
_____

author
_____

borrowed by
_____

date borrowed
_____

date returned
_____

title
_____

author
_____

borrowed by
_____

date borrowed
_____

date returned
_____

title

author

borrowed by

date borrowed

date returned

title

author

borrowed by

date borrowed

date returned

title

author

borrowed by

date borrowed

date returned

title

author

borrowed by

date borrowed

date returned

I have always come to life after coming to books.
Jorge Luis Borges (1899-1986)

title

author

borrowed by

date borrowed

date returned

title

author

borrowed by

date borrowed

date returned

title

author

borrowed by

date borrowed

date returned

title

author

borrowed by

date borrowed

date returned

title

author

borrowed by

date borrowed

date returned

title

author

borrowed by

date borrowed

date returned

title

author

borrowed by

date borrowed

date returned

FATHERS
AND SONS

*in which we find lists of books to give
as gifts and those books given to us*

give to

title

author

occasion

give to

title

author

occasion

give to

title

author

occasion

give to

title

author

occasion

If you caricature friends in your first novel they will be upset, but if you don't they will feel betrayed.

Mordecai Richler (1931-)

give to

title

author

occasion

give to

title

author

occasion

give to

title

author

occasion

give to

title

author

occasion

give to

title

author

occasion

give to

title

author

occasion

give to

title

author

occasion

give to

title

author

occasion

give to

title

author

occasion

give to

title

author

occasion

give to

title

author

occasion

give to

title

author

occasion

give to

title

author

occasion

give to

title

author

occasion

give to

title

author

occasion

Books are not rolls, to be devoured only when they are hot and fresh. A good book retains its interior heat and will warm a generation yet unborn.

Clifton Fadiman (1904-)

give to

title

author

occasion

give to

title

author

occasion

give to

title

author

occasion

give to

title

author

occasion

give to

title

author

occasion

give to

title

author

occasion

give to

title

author

occasion

give to

title

author

occasion

give to

title

author

occasion

give to

title

author

occasion

give to

title

author

occasion

give to

title

author

occasion

give to

title

author

occasion

give to

title

author

occasion

give to

title

author

occasion

give to

title

author

occasion

give to

title

author

occasion

give to

title

author

occasion

give to

title

author

occasion

give to

title

author

occasion

give to

title

author

occasion

give to

title

author

occasion

give to

title

author

occasion

give to

title

author

occasion

I wish thee as much pleasure in the reading,
as I had in the writing.

Francis Quarles (1592-1644)

give to

title

author

occasion

give to

title

author

occasion

give to

title

author

occasion

give to

title

author

occasion

given by
_____

title
_____

author
_____

occasion
_____

given by
_____

title
_____

author
_____

occasion
_____

given by
_____

title
_____

author
_____

occasion
_____

given by
_____

title
_____

author
_____

occasion
_____

given by
_____

title
_____

author
_____

occasion
_____

given by
_____

title
_____

author
_____

occasion
_____

given by
_____

title
_____

author
_____

occasion
_____

given by
_____

title
_____

author
_____

occasion
_____

given by
_____

title
_____

author
_____

occasion
_____

given by
_____

title
_____

author
_____

occasion
_____

give to

title

author

occasion

give to

title

author

occasion

give to

title

author

occasion

give to

title

author

occasion

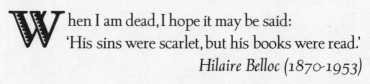

W hen I am dead, I hope it may be said:
'His sins were scarlet, but his books were read.'
Hilaire Belloc (1870-1953)

given by

title

author

occasion

given by

title

author

occasion

given by

title

author

occasion

given by

title

author

occasion

given by

title

author

occasion

given by

title

author

occasion

given by

title

author

occasion

given by

title

author

occasion

given by

title

author

occasion

given by

title

author

occasion

given by

title

author

occasion

given by

title

author

occasion

given by

title

author

occasion

given by

title

author

occasion

given by

title

author

occasion

'Tis the good reader that makes the good book.
Ralph Waldo Emerson (1803-82)

give to

title

author

occasion

give to

title

author

occasion

give to

title

author

occasion

give to

title

author

occasion

WHEN WE WERE VERY YOUNG

in which we remember our favourite
children's books, from youth and adulthood

There are only two or three human stories,
and they go on repeating themselves as
fiercely as if they had never happened before.
Willa Cather (1873-1974)

ON THE ROAD

in which we find a collection of books
suited for holidays, beaches and buses

I never travel without my diary.
One should always have something
sensational to read in the train.

Oscar Wilde (1854-1900)

Reading is to the mind what exercise is to the body.

Sir Richard Steele (1672-1759)

EX LIBRIS

FAR FROM THE MADDING CROWD

*in which we make note of book festivals,
author readings and other events for readers*

Reading is the work of an alert mind,
is demanding, and under ideal conditions
produces finally a sort of ecstasy.

E.B. White (1899-1985)

event

date/place

notes

event

date/place

notes

event

date/place

notes

event

date/place

notes

event

date/place

notes

event

date/place

notes

event

date/place

notes

event

date/place

notes

event

date/place

notes

event

date/place

notes

event

date/place

notes

event

date/place

notes

event

date/place

notes

event

date/place

notes

This is the Great Theatre of Life. Admission is free but the taxation is mortal. You come when you can, and leave when you must. The show is continuous. Good-night.

Robertson Davies (1913-95) from The Cunning Man

event

date/place

notes

event

date/place

notes

event

date/place

notes

event

date/place

notes

event

date/place

notes

event

date/place

notes

event

date/place

notes

event

date/place

notes

event

date/place

notes

A CIRCLE
OF FRIENDS

*in which we find a list of members of our reading club,
lists of books to read in a group and the thoughts
of the group on books read*

member	phone number	address

title   author

meeting date/time/place

title

author

members

notes

The liveliness of literature lies in its exceptionality, in being the individual, idiosyncratic vision of one human being, in which, to our delight and great surprise, we may find our own vision reflected.

Salman Rushdie (1947-)

meeting date/time/place

title

author

members

notes

meeting date/time/place

title

author

members

notes

meeting date/time/place

title

author

members

notes

meeting date/time/place

title

author

members

notes

meeting date/time/place

title

author

members

notes

The only important thing in a book is
the meaning it has for you.
W. Somerset Maugham (1874-1965)

meeting date/time/place

title

author

members

notes

meeting date/time/place

title

author

members

notes

meeting date/time/place

title

author

members

notes

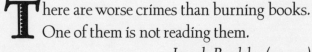

T here are worse crimes than burning books.
One of them is not reading them.

Joseph Brodsky (1940-)

meeting date/time/place

title

author

members

notes

meeting date/time/place

title

author

members

notes

THE MERCHANT
OF VENICE

*in which we find addresses of bookstores,
libraries, and book-loving friends*

name
_____

address
_____

phone
_____

notes
_____

name
_____

address
_____

phone
_____

notes
_____

name
_____

address
_____

phone
_____

notes
_____

name
_____

address
_____

phone
_____

notes
_____

> The magic of a bookstore stems in part from the depth of literature it contains, its surprises and mysteries ... A magical store has its own character and spirit.
>
> *Thomas Moore (1940-)*

name

address

phone

notes

name

address

phone

notes

name

address

phone

notes

name

address

phone

notes

name

address

phone

notes

name

address

phone

notes

name

address

phone

notes

name

address

phone

notes

name

address

phone

notes

name

address

phone

notes

name

address

phone

notes

name

address

phone

notes

name

address

phone

notes

name

address

phone

notes

name

address

phone

notes

Ith thought, patience, and discrimination, book passion becomes the signature of a person's character.

Nicholas A. Basbanes, A Gentle Madness

name

address

phone

notes

name

address

phone

notes

name

address

phone

notes

name

address

phone

notes

FAMOUS
LAST WORDS
in which we record memorable quotations
from favourite books and authors

The role of the writer is not to say what we
can all say, but what we are unable to say.

Anaïs Nin (1903-77)